THE LIBRARY OF HIP-HOP BIOGRAPHIES™

Russell Simmons

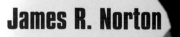

James R. Norton

The Rosen Publishing Group, Inc., New York

Published in 2006 by The Rosen Publishing Group, Inc.
29 East 21st Street, New York, NY 10010

Library of Congress Cataloging-in-Publication Data

Norton, James R.
Russell Simmons / by James R. Norton.—1st ed.
    p.cm.—(The library of hip-hop biographies)
Includes discography (p.   ) and bibliographical references (p.   ).
ISBN 1-4042-0515-2 (library binding)
1. Simmons, Russell. 2. Sound recording executives and producers—
United States—Biography. 3. Rap (Music)—History and criticism.
4. Def Jam Recordings. I. Title. II. Series.

ML429.S56N67 2006
782.421649'092—dc22

                                                        2005021293

Manufactured in the United States of America

On the cover: A 2003 portrait of Russell Simmons.

CONTENTS

INTRODUCTION

Hip-hop is more than just music. It's more than just a look, or an attitude. It's more than just two turntables and a microphone. It's more than just beats and rhymes.

Hip-hop is a complicated set of contradictions. It's flashy yet cool and understated. It's crude, and it's literate. It's about violence, and it's about peace. It's East Coast, and it's West Coast. It's also Southern. It's urban, it's suburban, and it's rural. It's American, and it's international. It's a community, and it's a mind-set. Hip-hop is a complicated, evolving organism.

Players in the world of hip-hop take on a wide variety of roles. They're rappers, or DJs, or producers, or critics, or street promoters, or financiers, or fans, or gangbangers living the life. Most of the people caught up in the world of hip-hop have seen at least a few of its facets firsthand. However, no one knows the story of hip-hop from more perspectives than Russell Simmons.

Born and raised in Queens, New York, Simmons was a cofounder of Def Jam Recordings, one of the labels that shaped hip-hop into the cultural force that it is today. Rubbing shoulders with original hip-hop pioneers such as Grandmaster Flash, Kurtis Blow, and Afrika Bambaataa, Simmons helped bring the art form from the New York underground scene to the American mainstream. Among the many names he helped make big are Public Enemy, the Beastie Boys, Run-D.M.C, and LL Cool J.

But he didn't stop there. Over the years, he's taken his career to the next level, making hundreds of millions of dollars as a record executive, television producer, and fashion mogul. Along the way, he has worked with the likes of Jay-Z, Donald Trump, Chris Tucker, and Jamie Foxx.

For most people, splitting time between being a music kingpin and a business leader would be enough. Not so for Simmons, who has taken his love of hip-hop into the realms of politics, art, and public service.

Throughout his many projects, Simmons has maintained a sense of personal pride and style that has helped him navigate the whirlwind of hip-hop's evolution. In his autobiography, *Life and Def: Sex, Drugs, Money + God*, he writes:

> I've never had dirty sneakers in my life. Not when I was a teenager and not now . . . [Sneakers] were a symbol of the pride I took in how I looked, which was crucial to my self-esteem—the same way certain sneakers, cars, or high-tech toys are for young people now. I've always understood that desire (because I used to think the same way), so I've never judged young people as harshly as many adults do. It's one of the ways I've managed to bridge the generation gap between my consumers and myself.

A yoga devotee and strict vegan, Simmons doesn't come off as a typical business kingpin. When *Fast Company* magazine caught up with him in November 2003, he was dressed in "floppy Phat Farm jeans, spotless white sneakers, a neon-green Polo shirt, and a pink Barbie Band-Aid behind his ear."

Beyond bridging the gap between the generations within the hip-hop community, Simmons has helped span the gaps between races, musical genres, and between the East Coast and the rest of the country. The story of Russell Simmons isn't just one of the richest stories in the world of hip-hop. It's one of the richest stories in the United States.

CHAPTER ONE

THE BIRTH OF HIP-HOP

Hip-hop is one of the world's most vital and power-ful cultural forces. A company trying to market its products to young people is likely to use hip-hop music and style in its commercials. Any film targeted at a young audience is likely to include hip-hop on its soundtrack. And event planners for any massive cultural event seeking a large youth audience have to consider getting hip-hop musicians involved.

This wasn't always the case. In the 1970s, hip-hop was just starting to find its voice in the New York club and house party scene. In the 1980s, it was a coastal thing, largely isolated in East and West Coast enclaves, reaching mostly urban audiences (with a few breakout hits). In the 1990s, hip-hop players such as the Notorious B.I.G., Dr. Dre, Tupac Shakur, Eminem, Warren G, and the Wu-Tang Clan blew the genre up to a new level of popularity and impact.

Modern hip-hop comes in many different flavors, from the hardest, bleakest gangsta rap to smooth G-funk to poetic, high-flying alternative hip-hop such as the recordings of De La Soul and Aesop Rock. But music historians tend to reach back to a simple old-school song to start telling hip-hop's story. That song, "Rapper's Delight," recorded by the Sugar Hill Gang in 1979, was the first straight-up hip-hop hit. When it came out, the track was seen as a flash in the pan, a one-hit novelty that would fade as fast as it had flared. Critics have since seen it as the dawn of a new musical era.

However, to young Russell Simmons and his peers, "Rapper's Delight" wasn't authentic, in part because the Sugar Hill Gang was a group put together by a recording studio, Sugar Hill Records. Moreover, the band was based in New Jersey—not New York City, where the clubs and house parties that drove hip-hop culture were primarily based.

ARTISTIC ROOTS, WILD BEGINNINGS

Born in 1957, Simmons grew up mostly in Hollis, Queens, a middle-class black neighborhood of New York City. His family moved there in 1965. As Simmons writes in *Life and Def*,

The release of the Sugar Hill Gang's "Rapper's Delight" marked a pivotal period in hip-hop history. Suddenly, everyone realized that hip-hop had the potential for wide commercial appeal. Despite the success of the record——and the band members' current status as pioneers and, even, legends——the Sugar Hill Gang was the object of sharp criticism and jealousy. To many of the b-boys and b-girls in the Bronx, the birthplace of the music, the band lacked street credibility.

Hollis, along with Jamaica and St. Albans, were Queens neighborhoods where black people from all over the city moved once they got a little change in their pockets. We had people from the projects in Brooklyn, the tenements in Harlem, and other parts of the city because you could own your own home with a loan from a credit union, giving you a feeling of suburban life while still within New York City.

His father, Daniel, was a schoolteacher and poet. His mother, Evelyn, was a recreation director for the New York City Department of Parks as well as a painter. They raised Simmons to appreciate the arts, although his father emphasized steady work and academic accomplishments.

Despite this, Simmons got caught up in the fast life of gangs and petty crime. Life in Hollis, though safer than many areas of New York City at the time, had its dangers and temptations. "As I entered adolescence in the early '70s," he writes in his autobiography, "heroin culture was a dominant part of life in Hollis, just as it was in similar working-class neighborhoods all over the country."

Simmons soon got pulled into the drug culture of the time. He sold marijuana and fake cocaine, and eventually became a warlord in the seventeenth division of a gang called the Seven Immortals. When he was sixteen, he shot at a stickup artist who had robbed him. Fortunately for Simmons and the robber—and for the development of hip-hop—the shot missed.

A NEW SCENE

Unlike many of those who join gangs, Simmons got out clean. After quitting gang life in 1975, he began attending the City College of New York (CCNY). While in school, Simmons caught a show by an MC called Eddie Cheeba. By modern standards, it was simple stuff—basic rhymes to encourage people to dance and make noise—but it blew Simmons's mind. Simmons writes in *Life and Def*:

I was standing there in a room full of peers—black and Hispanic college kids, partying and drinking—and it hit me: I wanted to be in this business . . . All the street entrepreneurship I'd learned selling herb, hawking fake cocaine, and staying out of jail, I decided to put into promoting music.

Simmons jumped into the game, renting venues and negotiating with acts in the burgeoning New York hip-hop scene. Soon, he was promoting full time, letting his schoolwork fall by the wayside. He left CCNY during his senior year, just a few credits away from a degree in sociology.

Although his father was angry with him for not completing his education, his mother supported his choice of career. After he went broke promoting a show, she gave him $2,000 out of her personal savings, allowing him to stay in the game. It was a rocky start to a great career.

At the time Simmons broke into hip-hop, the scene was loosely and poorly defined. Most MCs could DJ as well as rap. The breakdown between the roles of DJ and MC had not yet become a hard line, and the samples were from classic funk, jazz, and rock albums by musicians such as Bob James, James Brown, Eddie Kendricks, and the Incredible Bongo Band.

Simmons's first star, managed in tandem with his partner Rudy Toppin, was the MC Kurtis Blow, whose real name was Curtis Walker. The two met at CCNY, and it was Blow's low tenor voice and charisma that helped put Rush Management (as Simmons was billing himself) on the map.

FAMILY AND ROOTS

Russell Simmons's upbringing helped prepare him for his future role as a hip-hop bridge-builder between the worlds of black and white, urban and suburban, and rich and poor. He was raised amid the comfortable middle-class surroundings of Hollis, Queens. There he shared a bedroom with his younger brother, Joseph (later known as Run, of Run-D.M.C.). In *Life and Def*, Simmons describes his parents as worldly, creative people.

His dad was active in black empowerment and civil rights groups. Simmons writes about walking a picket line with his father to protest racial discrimination in housing and employment. His mother, raised in Queens by one of the first black nurses to work in New York City, is someone Simmons describes as a "real big-city woman . . . [with] some of the haughty attitude that can go with that in the black community."

Simmons's parents made sure that he was enrolled in P.S. 135, an integrated school in a working-class white neighborhood, instead of an overwhelmingly black school in Hollis. He described this as one of the best things that his parents ever did for him; it helped him realize, he writes, that "there are no differences between whites and blacks in terms of what they want out of life. Everybody wants to be liked."

Despite his stable family and comfortable surroundings, Simmons and his older brother, Danny, got a firsthand taste of crime while growing up. Simmons spent time in "the game," the world of gangs, guns and drugs that is the backdrop for so much of the modern hip-hop scene. A run-in with drug-related violence and the social scene at CCNY helped bring Simmons out of the world of crime, and into the world of music.

Soon Simmons and his acts, including Blow, were working the Manhattan track of clubs and other venues. The audiences on this track were easier to please than those at other concerts, because every show was also a party. They danced, drank, and talked, and they listened to the performances.

Simmons quickly began to pick up on one of the basic lessons of his lifelong career—originality and authenticity were the keys to success. He realized that it was important to tap into the performer's true identity and to amplify it, instead of following the fash-

Born in Harlem in 1959, Kurtis Blow rose up the ranks of the hip-hop community to become its first superstar. He started out as a break-dancer then worked as a club DJ before he started rapping. His breakout tune "The Breaks" was the first rap record to sell more than 500,000 copies.

ions and marketing tactics of already successful acts. In the case of many of Simmons's acts, he learned to emphasize their ghetto credibility rather than mimic rock stars.

Simmons also realized that aggressive branding and promoting were just as important as staying true to one's roots. Accordingly, he took Kurtis Blow into Queens, where the competition wasn't nearly as strong as it was in Manhattan, and where

Russell Simmons began his hip-hop career as a concert promoter. Tapping into the street smarts he picked up as a drug dealer and the lessons he learned from early failures, he developed his own marketing approach to nurture hip-hop's undefined market. He is pictured here backstage at the Paramount Theatre in Seattle, Washington, before a performance by Run-D.M.C. on June 17, 1987.

Blow's Harlem roots gave him an aura of glamour and celebrity. Simmons also teamed Blow with Grandmaster Flash and the Furious Five, a legendary team of MCs, giving Blow another dose of much-needed credibility. When Blow had a hit record in 1979 ("Christmas Rappin'") the pressure was on, and Simmons's career was ready to hit a new level.

CHAPTER TWO

FROM UNDERGROUND TO BIG TIME

In the early 1980s, after years of working hip-hop at the street level, things began to click for Simmons. He was starting to push hip-hop culture beyond its black, urban roots onto a central cultural stage where it could be experienced by Americans of all races and classes.

Simmons's career took a fateful turn in 1984, when he teamed up with New York University student Rick Rubin to create the Def Jam label. They made an unusual duo. Rubin, a punk-rock fan from a well-to-do Jewish family, and Simmons, a black

Rick Rubin (back row, second from right) poses with Russell Simmons (front row, right), Run-D.M.C., and a producer on the set of *Tougher Than Leather*, a 1988 movie that Rubin cowrote and directed. He was one of the main architects of the early Def Jam sound.

former gangbanger and club promoter, came from different ends of the music world. But they both had a sense of street aesthetic, a lust for breaking through to big audiences, and a talent for finding talent. They would form a hardcore duo in the years to come: Rubin crafting stripped-down, hard-rock inspired jams and edgy logos and graphics, while Simmons networked and built a business empire.

THE SIMMONS STYLE

The Simmons philosophy, as it has evolved over dozens of years, dozens of bands, and dozens of business ventures, has three constant themes. They are:

Keep it real, and the audience comes to you. Too many performers, according to Simmons, are groomed to look and sound like whatever's popular. The acts that hit it big and stick around are the ones that are true to their roots. Listeners can pick up on phoniness, and they won't be loyal to an act with a paper-thin story and a corporate-designed look. Def Jam groups tend to stick around for a long time. "Unlike Motown," writes Simmons in *Life and Def*, "I don't believe in catering to the so-called mainstream by altering your look or slang or music. I see hip-hop culture as the new American mainstream. We don't change for you; you adapt to us."

Don't hold grudges. Though it's tempting to feud with those who have burned you on a deal, Simmons argues it's just bad for business. For example, he once did business with a promoter named Saint James. Simmons gave him $1,900 to promote a show, and Saint James just disappeared with it. Simmons was mad. But as his business expanded, he needed street-smart music people like Saint James, so he gave him a job. "I try very hard not to hold grudges," Simmons writes in *Life and Def*. "The guy you hate today could easily be working for you tomorrow. If you stick around long enough in this business, everything comes full circle."

Get out of the office. Simmons is renowned for doing business on the road and in the streets, cell phone in hand. "Everything worth knowing in this business happens outside the building," Simmons writes in *Life and Def*. "Eventually I got to know everybody who was a player, because once I had a hot record they had to call me. No one cared who I was, what I wore or even what my records sounded like if I had something they wanted."

Simmons got his first real chance to bring all his skills to bear in the newly formed Def Jam Recordings. Working together with Rubin, he helped bring about the dawn of big-time, mainstream hip-hop.

RUN-D.M.C.

One of Simmons's first breakout acts was Run-D.M.C., a group composed of Darryl McDaniels (D.M.C.), Jason Mizell (Jam Master Jay), and Joseph Simmons (Run), Russell Simmons's younger brother. Although Run-D.M.C. didn't record on Def Jam, it was handled by Russell Simmons's management group, Rush Management.

Run-D.M.C.'s first appearance before a proper hip-hop crowd was a disaster. Booked at the Disco Fever club in the Bronx in the spring of 1983, the group was overdressed and missing Jam Master Jay, whose ride had never turned up. Alex Ogg tells the story of the concert in *The Men Behind Def Jam*:

The MCing duo were then greeted with gales of laughter as they took the stage. It was bad enough that these hip hop pretenders hailed from the Queens (considered "soft" by Bronx residents), but their checkered sports jackets did not impress anyone—DMC had actually borrowed his suit from his father's wardrobe. He was so humiliated by the experience that he almost gave up the idea of being a rapper on the spot.

However, Run-D.M.C. bounced back with a vengeance. The trio moved away from flamboyant showbiz costumes and started wearing "street" clothes on the stage. Soon, they had nailed down a look—leather suits, black velour fedoras, and gold chains. And with the single "Rock Box," in 1983, the band broke into MTV rotation and started down the trailblazing path of merging rock guitar riffs with clear, forceful hip-hop lyrics.

Simmons nurtured the group, getting it signed to a medium-sized independent record label and helping to set up lucrative tours that took advantage of Run-D.M.C.'s relatively small size and minimal equipment needs.

Released in 1986, Run-D.M.C.'s third album, *Raising Hell*, was a disc that helped lay the template for countless rap albums to follow. It had a lot of now-familiar hip-hop mainstays, such as product shout-outs ("My Adidas"), black-power rhymes ("Proud to Be Black") and the rock-rap crossover of "Walk This Way."

It was "Walk This Way" that hammered the group into America's consciousness. Recorded with the rock group

19

Aerosmith, "Walk This Way" was a musical duel between the new, urban hip-hop and the familiar, suburban rock. It caught on like wildfire, breaking hip-hop to a new audience and resurrecting the flagging career of Aerosmith in the process.

THE YOUNG AND THE LUCRATIVE

One of Def Jam's first breakout groups was the Beastie Boys, a team of arrogant knuckleheads with an unmatchable sense of swagger and a flair for tight, hilarious rhymes. Adam Horovitz (known as Adrock in the Beastie Boys) was originally in a punk band called the Young and the Useless. But in 1984, he switched over to hip-hop full-time, joining Beastie Boys Michael Diamond (Mike D) and Adam Yauch (MCA).

Simmons was an early mentor to the group, although the Beastie Boys and Def Jam would angrily part ways after the 1986 release of *Licensed to Ill*. Music writers have observed that Simmons's relationship with the Beastie Boys is one of the few examples of a black producer helping white musicians find their way through a traditionally black genre. Simmons and Rubin saw the potential that the Beastie Boys had to reach fans across the board, and viewed them as a smart investment.

The Beastie Boys had a big impact. The group was the first great cross-racial success story in hip-hop. Its first breakout hit, "Fight for Your Right" hit the mainstream music scene like an atom bomb. Written as a joke, it wasn't the band's choice for a single when *Licensed to Ill* was released. However, it exploded on to the

Run-D.M.C. and the Beastie Boys pose for a publicity shot at an unspecified location during the *Raising Hell* tour in 1986. In the front row, from left to right, are Mike D, Jam Master Jay, Adrock, and Run. In the back row, from left to right, are DJ Hurricane (the Beastie Boys' DJ), MCA, and Darryl McDaniels of Run-D.M.C.

radio and MTV, capturing the sound of teenage rebellion with its loud, shallow, confrontational flavor.

Simmons included the Beastie Boys on Run-D.M.C.'s *Raising Hell* tour, where the all-white group won over audiences of all races. Describing the reception of the Beastie Boys on the tour in his autobiography, Simmons writes:

> *The predominantly black audience wasn't racist about it at all. They were like "Yo, that's the white boys." In a pack*

of acts they stood out. They played in front of black audiences and no one really cared in a negative way . . . They were ultimately accepted by black people because they were good.

Despite the Beastie Boys' initial success, it parted on bad terms with Simmons and Rubin, severing its ties to Def Jam after *Licensed to Ill*. A fight over royalties withheld by Simmons—and a drastic drop in the Beastie Boys' productivity—was at the heart of the dispute. Simmons's business-driven mind-set and the recklessness of the young Beastie Boys had collided head-on.

FIGHTING THE POWER

At the same time that the Beastie Boys were crashing through racial barriers and rocking MTV, Def Jam was developing one of the most important music groups that the United States has seen. With its political themes, unchecked anger, verbal brilliance, and militant black pride, Public Enemy forever changed the way hip-hop was viewed.

In its heyday, Public Enemy was unapologetic about blaring its urgent revolutionary messages that protested racial discrimination and promoted black power. The group was often demonized by the media and many government officials, and was even singled out in an FBI report on rap music and national security. Its two front men, Flavor Flav (left) and Chuck D are pictured here performing at a concert in the New York City area around 1991.

The group's roster has changed over time, but at the height of its popularity on Def Jam, it was made up of front man and main vocalist Chuck D (Carlton Ridenhour), vocalist Flavor Flav (William Drayton), choreographer and "minister of information" Professor Griff (Richard Griffin), and DJ Terminator X (Norman Rogers).

Public Enemy's tracks directly addressed racial and political issues in a way that left many white, conservative media commentators feeling threatened and many young urban listeners feeling liberated. One of the group's biggest hits, "911 Is a Joke" attacked the slow response rate of emergency services in poor, urban neighborhoods. It goes, in part:

> Everyday they don't never come correct
> You can ask my man right here with the broken neck
> He's a witness to the job never bein' done
> He would've been in full effect
> But late 911 was a joke 'cause they always jokin'
> They the token to your life when it's croakin'
> They need to be in a pawn shop on a
> 911 is a joke we don't want 'em

By protecting and promoting the group when it was confronting the very culture that surrounded it, Simmons helped redefine the scope of hip-hop. "Public Enemy," writes Simmons in *Life and Def*, "was the most important act in Def Jam history because they epitomized the label's sound and the merger of two cultures—hip-hop and rock."

CASHING IN

Simmons and Rubin founded Def Jam before its genre was even fully hatched. Under Simmons's leadership, it became the world's hip-hop pace-setter, racking up albums by the millions. But the label is known for more than its hip-hop sales. Its reach extended into the worlds of video games, comedy, and movies. Among others, the Def Jam label launched the careers of LL Cool J, Slick Rick, Warren G, DMX, Onyx, Ashanti, and Jay-Z, defining the sound of both old-school and 1990s hip-hop in the process.

In a business famous for one-hit wonders, fast rises, and hard tumbles, Def Jam showed an amazing longevity and resilience. It led the initial charge to establish hip-hop as a major commercial genre in the mid-1980s, and then bounced back in the mid-1990s after a post-1980s lull.

Although Rubin and other talent-sensitive executives deserve most of the credit for serving as scouts for Def Jam's talent, it was invariably Simmons who provided the organization's public face and relentless engine of entrepreneurial energy. Simmons constantly hit the road, making critical networking connections that expanded Def Jam's reach and contacts. He pushed Def Jam's tentacles into new markets and mediums with the aggressive drive of a visionary.

Simmons gained full ownership of Def Jam in 1988, when Rubin left the label to form the Def American label, now American Recordings. In 1993, Simmons sold 60 percent of Def Jam for $33 million. Six years later, he sold his remaining interest in the

A SELECTED DEF JAM DISCOGRAPHY

LL COOL J
Radio (1985)
Bigger and Deffer (1987)
Mama Said Knock You Out
(1990)

BEASTIE BOYS
Licensed to Ill (1986)

PUBLIC ENEMY
*It Takes a Nation of Millions to
Hold Us Back* (1988)
Fear of a Black Planet (1990)

REDMAN
Whut? Thee Album (1992)

METHOD MAN
Tical (1994)

WARREN G
Regulate . . . . G Funk Era (1994)
Take a Look over Your Shoulder
(1997)

JAY-Z
Reasonable Doubt (1996)
In My Lifetime Vol. 1 (1997)
Vol. 2: Hard Knock Life (1998)
Vol. 3: Life and Times of S. Carter
(1999)

FOXY BROWN
Ill Na Na (1996)
Chyna Dolla (1998)

DMX
It's Dark and Hell Is Hot (1998)
*Flesh of My Flesh, Blood of My
Blood* (1998)

Despite his seemingly laid-back personality and management style, Russell Simmons, shown here in his office at Def Jam in April 2003, is an ambitious and aggressive businessman who works tirelessly to achieve his goal.

company to Seagram's Universal Music Group for $100 million. Nevertheless, he remains chairman of the company.

Around the time of the sale, Def Jam's market share in the powerful hip-hop sector of the music industry stood at close to 30 percent. This is an awesome achievement not just for Def Jam within the world of hip-hop, but for any music label within any genre.

CHAPTER THREE

BUSINESS BOOMS

If Simmons had gone into a quiet retirement after selling Def Jam in 1999, he would still be remembered as one of the founders and pioneers of hip-hop. But he has always aggressively branched out into new ventures, becoming one of the most visible entrepreneurs in American history and breaking through social and financial barriers in the process.

There have traditionally been two models for black cultural businesses in America. The first, as typified by magazines like *Ebony* or *Essence*, concentrates on black writers, editors, and producers creating products for black readers and consumers. The second, as typified by record producer Berry Gordy's Motown label, took music written and performed by blacks and marketed it to anyone who would listen.

Simmons, as he writes in *Life and Def*, takes a third approach: "My core audience, my hip-hop audience, is black and white, Asian and Hispanic—anyone who totally identifies with and lives in the culture. Those are my peeps."

Any project that hits a hip-hop audience is potentially attractive to Simmons. (He's even marketed an energy drink, DefCon3, which made its debut at the end of 2004.) But his forays into fashion, television, and Hollywood have captured the most attention.

Comedy Goes Def

In 1991, Simmons helped launch *Def Comedy Jam*, a project that would give him a vital sideline to his still-thriving involvement in the music business. The televised comedy tour was initially a collaboration between two black men (Simmons and TV executive Stan Lathan) and two white men (Bernie Brillstein and Brad Grey of the management company Brillstein-Grey).

Def Comedy Jam was originally inspired by performances at the Comedy Act Theater in Los Angeles, California, which in turn echoed the sometimes raunchy, often racially provocative comedy that the original "chitlin' circuit" of black comedy clubs once fostered. First broadcast on HBO in 1991, it was a natural

Comedian Martin Lawrence poses with Russell Simmons at a taping of *Def Comedy Jam* in 1994. Lawrence, who made his film debut in Spike Lee's *Do the Right Thing* in 1989, remains one of the most prominent African American comedic actors.

for Simmons. There were many similarities between managing stand-up comics and managing rappers. Both types of entertainers often raged against the powers that be, challenging their listeners, and speaking up for the concerns of young people. Both types of entertainers were also cheap to manage, relatively speaking—all a rapper or a stand-up needs onstage is a microphone and a sound system.

Originally hosted by Martin Lawrence, and featuring a lineup that, over time, included Bernie Mac, Bill Bellamy, Jamie Foxx, and Chris Tucker, *Def Comedy Jam* ranged from family-friendly jokes, to angry political satire, to the "blue" (dirty) humor for which the show was often criticized. Critic Nelson George put the impact of *Def Comedy Jam* into perspective in *Hip-Hop America*:

> The Def Comedy Jam *changed the game . . . The weekly thirty-minute broadcast gave a national platform to scores of otherwise little-known comics, leading to a wave of*

interest that would overflow into the movies, TV, and commercials . . . The top Def Comedy Jam *performers ended up flowing into everything from MTV to sitcoms, from voice-overs to headlining their own tours.*

It also helped establish Simmons's credentials as a television producer, a talent he continues to exercise. At the end of 2004, the Simmons Lathan Media Group and Clear Channel Entertainment Television announced an agreement to produce twelve music- and fashion-related events per year under the banner Def on Demand.

On the heels of the successful *Def Comedy Jam*, Simmons created *Def Poetry Jam* in 2002. The series debuted on HBO, showcasing the creative skills of poets, rappers, comedians, and other spoken-word artists.

FROM TRACKS TO TRACKSUITS

Hip-hop has always been about more than just the music. From square one, fashion has played a key role in the scene. Fashion speaks to a player's style, status, class, roots, and aspirations. The right clothes can make or break a career, a lesson Simmons learned early.

By 1992, Simmons had become a power player in all aspects of hip-hop—the music, the fashion, and the life. He had connections with many of the hottest artists, and a good pool of money with which to work. He was poised to take the next step and build on his stature.

Russell Simmons, shown here in a showroom at Phat Farm's headquarters, was the first hip-hop personality to launch a fashion line. The inset photo shows his wife Kimora Lee, waving to the crowd as she walked the runway with their daughter at the end of her Baby Phat fall collection show in New York City on February 13, 2003.

Founding the Phat Farm fashion house was that logical next move. Phat Farm's first retail store opened in Manhattan in 1993. Its designs were inspired by the styles of the street, such as hooded sweatshirts, baggy jeans, and the prominent display of a fashion-house logo.

The brand's explosive success led to the founding of the Baby Phat line for women in 2000. This time, however, it wasn't Simmons who did the founding and management—it was his wife, Kimora Lee. That, in turn, led to two children's lines, Phat Farm Boys and Baby Phat Girlz. The fashion house also came out with a fragrance called Premium in 2001 and the Phat Classic Sneaker in 2002. Over the past decade, Phat Farm has grown from a $500,000 boutique business to a $500 million plus lifestyle collection sporting items including jewelry, eyewear, bags, suits, and accessories.

SIMMONS AND THE SILVER SCREEN

Less lucrative but equally glamorous to Simmons's careers in music, television, and fashion is his career on and behind the scenes of the big screen. His first foray was the 1985 film *Krush Groove*, the fictionalized story of Def Jam's early years. It starred hip-hop artists including Run-D.M.C., the Fat Boys, Rick Rubin, and Kurtis Blow. Simmons co-produced the film but played only a bit part onscreen. Actor Blair Underwood played the major character based on Simmons.

Simmons and Rubin decided the final product was too light-weight, and lined up support to produce *Tougher Than Leather*, a 1988 film about Run-D.M.C. tracking down the drug lord/record company executive who murdered their friend. The low-budget, cheesy final product convinced Simmons to stay out of movies for a while.

He got back into the game in 1996 as a producer of *The Nutty Professor*, which starred Eddie Murphy as a half-dozen different characters, including Professor Sherman Klump.

Krush Groove, a still from which is shown here, was Russell Simmons's first film venture. Made on a budget of approximately $3 million, the movie grossed more than $11 million at the box office.

Simmons scored $600,000 for his work on the film ("Nothing by Hollywood standards," he writes in *Life and Def*). However, he clashed with Brian Grazer, a powerful movie industry insider. Hollywood left a sour taste in the Queens, New York, native's mouth.

CHAPTER FOUR

ACTIVISM, ELECTION 2004, AND BEYOND

Despite his many accomplishments as a businessman, Simmons has always been about more than dollars and cents. On top of all his other projects, he has launched himself into politics and social activism.

A NEW KIND OF CARD

Simmons founded UniRush in 2003 to offer financial services to the estimated 48 million Americans outside of traditional banking. One of the central initiatives of UniRush was the Rush card, a joint venture with Visa.

People who don't have a traditional bank account can use Rush cards to receive payments such as tax returns or paychecks, instead of using expensive check-cashing services. The card has attracted 500,000 customers since its launch in 2003.

In 2005, UniRush teamed up with Intuit (the maker of Turbo Tax software) to launch a Web site designed to make it easier for young adults to claim tax refunds. It allows its users to file their tax returns on the Web for a $5.95 fee, and receive a refund within ten days.

HIP-HOPPING THE VOTE

Among his other projects, Simmons cofounded the Hip-Hop Summit Action Network, a coalition of hip-hop artists, entertainment leaders, civil rights proponents, and youth leaders dedicated to fighting poverty and injustice.

During the 2004 presidential election, the Hip-Hop Summit Action Network held twenty-six hip-hop summits featuring artists Kanye West and 50 Cent, among others. Its goal was to persuade young people to vote. In the 2004 presidential race, 21 million voters aged thirty or younger came to the polls. This represented a jump of 4.6 million votes, or an increase of 2 percent of the overall vote as compared to 2000, for which political observers gave Simmons a lot of credit.

Simmons has also campaigned for a scale-back of New York State's tough mandatory drug sentencing laws, known as the Rockefeller drug laws. The laws imposed mandatory sentences

Russell Simmons (wearing a baseball cap) smiles as he watches New York governor George Pataki sign a bill reforming the Rockefeller drug laws at a news conference on December 14, 2004.

to even minor offenders, regardless of their background. For example, the possession of four ounces or sale of two ounces of certain controlled substances was a class A felony that warranted a sentence of fifteen years to life in prison—a stricter sentence than that imposed on most people convicted of rape, robbery, or manslaughter.

A partial repeal of the law, signed by Govenor George Pataki in December 2004, eliminated the maximum term of life in prison for the most serious drug offenses, and changed a common sentence of three years to life to a sentence of three years. Pataki was quoted by the Associated Press as saying: "With the signing of this law today, these offenders will be given another chance to lead a productive life free of drugs and crime." Simmons attended the signing ceremony.

THE BIG PICTURE

After a still-booming career that has thrived for more than twenty-five years, Simmons is both defiant and proud of what he's accomplished. "The arrogance of white men is why I'm here today," said Simmons in a 2004 interview with *CBS News*. "If it weren't for them, I wouldn't be here. What the hell did they need me for if they were open-minded enough to allow this cultural phenomena to be part of their make-up. My independence is because they didn't accept me."

In *Life and Def*, Simmons writes about his *Def Poetry Jam* program. In the process, he puts out a statement that can be applied to what the hip-hop movement stands for:

> *Every significant political movement in the world has been energized by the spirit of young people, and right now a lot of them have become apathetic, through no fault of their own. However, we can't move forward as a country without them. It's the young people who need to tell us how to fix the mess that old people have made. What young people need is a platform for their ideas and an*

outlet to get involved with in the process of political and social change.

From the 1970s until the present day, while starting dozens of new ventures and making hundreds of millions of dollars, Simmons has built that platform for young people dollar by dollar, and track by track. Under Simmons's guidance, the Def Jam label put out some of the most important records in hip-hop history. The label put hip-hop on the popular music charts in the mid- to late-1980s. In addition, Russell

Russell Simmons announces the launch of the Russell Simmons Music Group at a press conference in New York City on April 13, 2005. Rapper Jay-Z, who is also the president and CEO of Def Jam Recordings, looks on.

Simmons's management group, the now defunct Rush Management, handled the careers of hip-hop artists including Kurtis Blow, Run-D.M.C., and DJ Jazzy Jeff and the Fresh Prince. Though the decades fly by, Simmons stays in the game.

TIMELINE

1957   Russell Simmons is born in Queens, New York.

1983   Simmons helps cofound and produce pioneering rap group Run-D.M.C.

1984   Def Jam Recordings is cofounded by Simmons and Rick Rubin.

1986   Run-D.M.C. and Aerosmith break down the wall between rock and rap with their remix of "Walk This Way."

1987   The Beastie Boys album *Licensed to Ill*, released by Def Jam, becomes rap's first number one album.

1990   A lucrative deal with Sony Records provides Simmons with enough money to fund Rush Communications, his ticket into ventures such as movies and fashion.

1991   Simmons begins producing *Def Comedy Jam* on HBO.

1992   Simmons starts the young urban apparel line Phat Farm.

1996   Simmons launches *One World* magazine.

1998   Simmons marries model Kimora Lee.

1999   Simmons sells his share of Def Jam to the Universal Music Group for $100 million.

2000	Daughter Ming Lee is born to Russell and Kimora Lee Simmons.
2001	Simmons forms the Hip-Hop Summit Action Network to boost political and social activism among the younger members of the hip-hop generation.
2002	Daughter Aoki Lee is born to Russell and Kimora Lee Simmons.
2002	HBO launches a series of *Def Poetry Jam* programs.
2004	Simmons announces his "Get Your House in Order" financial empowerment and home ownership readiness initiative.
2004	Simmons mobilizes young voters through his Hip-Hop Summit Action Network group.
2004	The Russell Simmons Beverage Company introduces the DefCon3 energy drink.
2004	Prompted in part by lobbying from Simmons, New York governor George Pataki signs legislation to scale back the state's tough and inflexible mandatory sentences for drug offenses.
2005	Simmons's financial services company, UniRush, teams up with Intuit to launch a Web site to make it easier for young adults to claim tax refunds.

GLOSSARY

DJ An abbreviation for "disc jockey." Also known as turntablism. It's the art of using a record player as a musical instrument, using techniques such as cutting, scratching, and needle drops. Also, the person who plays the accompanying music for the rapper who plays recorded music for an audience, such as at a party of a club.

hip-hop A cultural movement that began among urban African American youth in New York City. It has since spread around the world, incorporating elements such as MCing, DJing, graffiti, breaking, beatboxing, political activism, hip-hop fashion, and hip-hop slang.

MC An abbreviation for "master of ceremonies," or "mic controller," it's the title given to the vocal performer on a rap track.

rap To speak lyrics in sync to a rhythm. Along with DJing, rapping is a part of hip-hop music.

sampling The act of taking part of one sound recording and reusing it as an element of a new recording.

FOR MORE INFORMATION

The Hip-Hop Archive at the W. E. B. Du Bois Institute
   for Afro-American Research
Department of Afro-American Studies
12 Quincy Street
Barker Center, 2nd Floor
Cambridge, MA 02138
(617) 495-4113
Web site: http://www.hiphoparchive.org

Web Sites

Due to the changing nature of Internet links, the Rosen Publishing Group, Inc., has developed an online list of Web sites related to the subject of this book. This site is updated regularly. Please use this link to access the list:

http://www.rosenlinks.com/lhhb/rusi

FOR FURTHER READING

Cepeda, Raquel, ed. *And It Don't Stop: The Best American Hip-Hop Journalism of the Last 25 Years*. New York, NY: Faber & Faber, 2004.

Forman, Murray. *The 'Hood Comes First: Race, Space, and Place in Rap and Hip-Hop*. Middletown, CT: Wesleyan University Press, 2002.

Forman, Murray, and Mark Anthony Neal, eds. *That's the Joint! The Hip-Hop Studies Reader*. New York, NY: Routledge, 2004.

Ogg, Alex. *The Men Behind Def Jam: The Radical Rise of Russell Simmons And Rick Rubin*. New York, NY: Omnibus Press, 2002.

BIBLIOGRAPHY

Butler, Desmond. "New York Governor Signs Measure Scaling
   Back Mandatory Sentences for Drug Offenses," Associated
   Press, December 14, 2004.

Carberry, Maegan. "Russell's World," *The Chicago Tribune*
   RedEye Edition, October 26, 2004.

Cohen, Eric. "Beastie Boys to Men: A Retrospective," *The Ottawa
   Citizen*, November 6, 2004.

Eldredge, Richard L. "Hip-Hop Godfather Touts All Things Def,"
   The Atlanta Journal-Constitution, October 22, 2004.

Gamboa, Glen. "30 Years of Hip-Hop," *Newsday*,
   October 14, 2004.

George, Nelson. *Hip-hop America*. New York, NY: Viking
   Penguin, 1998.

Hahn, Lucinda. "As Fundraiser, 'Simmons' Gets Good Rap," *The
   Chicago Tribune*, October 25, 2004.

Heldenfels, R. D. "As Rap Celebrates 30 Years, Russell Simmons
   Wants Credibility for Hip-Hop," *Akron Beacon Journal*,
   October 3, 2004.

Kapner, Suzanne. "Simmons Goes Into Refund Biz," *New York
   Post*, January 27, 2005.

Kurtz, Rod. "America's 25 Most Fascinating Entrepreneurs:
   Russell Simmons," *Inc.*, April 1, 2004.

Light, Alan, ed. *The Vibe Story of Hip-Hop*. New York, NY: Three Rivers Press, 1999.

Ogg, Alex. *The Men Behind Def Jam: The Radical Rise of Russell Simmons and Rick Rubin*. New York, NY: Omnibus Press, 2002.

Perkins, Ken Parish. "'Def' Becomes Him," *Fort Worth Star Telegram*, October 3, 2004.

Petrocelli, Michael. "Hip-Hopper Makes Voting a Thing to Do," *The Durham Herald-Sun*, October 29, 2004.

Reingold, Jennifer. "Rush Hour," *Fast Company*, November 2003.

Rose, Charlie. "Russell Simmons, Unplugged," *CBS News*, February 11, 2004.

Simmons, Russell. *Life and Def: Sex, Drugs, Money + God*. New York, NY: Three Rivers Press, 2001.

Stark, Jeff. "Salon Brilliant Careers: Russell Simmons," *Salon*, July 6, 1999.

"They Made America—Innovators—Russell Simmons," PBS Web Site. Retrieved April 2005 (http://www.pbs.org/wgbh/theymadeamerica/filmmore/s4.html).

Vargas, Jose Antonio. "Vote or Die? Well, They Did Vote," *Washington Post*, November 9, 2004.

Willis, Gerri. "Russell Simmons Says, 'Get Your House in Order,'" *CNN Financial News*, November 5, 2004.

INDEX

ABOUT THE AUTHOR

James Norton graduated from the University of Wisconsin in 1999 with a degree in history. While an undergraduate, he edited the *Daily Cardinal*, and founded *Flak* magazine, which focuses on the "review and criticism" of popular culture, politics, and the media. He currently lives in Cambridge, Massachusetts.

PHOTO CREDITS

Cover, p. 27 © James Leynse/Corbis; p.1 © Getty Images, Inc.; p. 9 © The Michael Ochs Archives; pp. 13, 30, 34 © The Everett Collection; p. 16 © New Line Cinema/ Photofest; pp. 21, 23 © Lynn Goldsmith/Corbis; p. 32 © AP/Wide World Photo; p. 32 (inset) © Reuters/Corbis; p. 37 © Ramin Talaie/Corbis; p. 39 © Chip East/ Reuters/Corbis.

Designer: Thomas Forget; Editor: Wayne Anderson